Al-Shabaab: The Threat To Kenya And The Horn Of Africa

Al Shabaab, which means 'the youth" or "the boys" in Arabic is a militant Islamist group founded and based in Somalia. The group has waged an insurgency against the Transitional Federal Government as well as the African Union (AU) peace keeping force, the African Mission in Somalia (AMISOM). Al Shabaab began as part of the armed wing of the Islamic Courts Union (ICU) when the Courts Union gained power in the Somali capital of Mogadishu in 2006, then the Ethiopian Forces intervened to root them out, and the leadership went into exile[1]. The fighters, however, remained in the country and fought the Ethiopians until they withdrew in 2009. Since then, they have remained a formidable militia force with the capability to conduct terror attacks in neighboring Kenya and across into Uganda, which is an indication of their threat capability. Somalia remains one of the world's worst humanitarian situations today since the fall of dictator Mohamed Said Barre in 1991, and combined with the frequent drought and famine, coupled with the brutal conflict between al Shabaab and government forces supported by AMISOM forces, makes the Horn of Africa region a security hotspot.

The ouster of al Shabaab by the Kenya Defense Forces (KDF) and AMISOM, from their stronghold in the south and central portions of Somalia, especially the port city of Kisumayo and Mogadishu, was a major milestone and a turning point in the influence of the militia group's operations in Somalia and a starting point on the road to the strategic component of degrading threats to peace and stability in the Horn of Africa region to enable the nurturing of democracy and the proper exploitation of natural resources, economic development, and capacity building necessary to improve the quality of life for people in a secure environment. In this strategic research project, I will present the historic background and demography of Somalia, the genesis of al Shabaab and its operations, look at the threat posed by the militia group to Kenya and the Horn of Africa region at large, as well as the strategic implications for Kenya and discuss Kenya's current strategy. The paper will also highlight current efforts, from a military perspective, and the strategies to mitigate the threat posed by al Shabaab. Finally I will conclude with recommendations for the way forward.

Historic Background and Demography of Somalia

The Somalia Republic gained independence on 1st July 1960 formed by the Union of British Somaliland and Italian Somaliland with Aden Abdullah Osman as its first elected President. Nine years later a socialist state was formed following a coup organized by Major General Mohamed Said Barre. In 1991 rebel forces ousted the Barre regime due to its authoritarian rule characterized by the persecution, imprisonment, and torture of political opponents.[2] Since the departure of Barre hunger, turmoil, factional fighting and the lack of a stable functional, central and credible government, has led Somalia to be regarded as a failed state.[3] In May 1991 northern clans within Somalia declared Somaliland an independent republic with a functioning administration, which has not subsequently been recognized by any members of the international community except Ethiopia. In 1998 the regions of northeastern Somalia centered on Garowe in the Nagaal province declared the territory an autonomous state called the Puntland State of Somalia. However, Puntland is not trying to obtain international recognition as a separate nation.[4]

Somalia borders Kenya to the southwest, Ethiopia to the west, and Eritrea and Djibouti to the northwest. It is bounded by the Red Sea to the north and Indian Ocean to the east.[5] The population is estimated to be 10,085,638 (July 2012 est.) made up of eighty five percent Somali, fifteen percent Bantu and five percent other ethnic groups. The languages spoken are Somali (official), Arabic (official), English, and Italian. Sunni Islam is the official religion while Sufi Islam, which is a moderate mystical form of Islam, is also practiced.[6] Despite the lack of an effective system of governance, the economy of Somali is largely based on remittance money transfers, raising livestock, the production of leather, fishing, charcoal production and the cultivation of bananas.[7] Somali society is oriented around strong kinship networks that often serve as a source of protection, security, and patronage. The kinship structure is based on an agnatic lineage known as clan. The lineage of the pastoral Somalis are united by a common mythological perception of direct lineal descent from their forefather Samaal and the household of the Prophet Mohammed, notably the Qurayshi clan, and specifically his cousin, Aqiil Bin Abi Talib.[8]

The four main clan families are the Darood who are divided into the Ogaden, Marehan and Harti mainly found in Puntland and the Gedo region of lower Juba. They are also found in Ethiopia and Kenya. The Hawiye are divided into the Habar, Gedir, and Abgaal. They are mostly found in central and southern Somalia and dominant in Mogadishu. The Ajuraan and Abgaal are often seen as part of the Hawiye. The Dir include groups such as the Issa, Gadabursi, and Biymaal. They are found in Somaliland as well as in south central Somalia. The Isaaq, sometimes in dispute as to whether they constitute a clan family or are a part of the Dir, are found in Somaliland.

The other clans are the agro-pastoralist groups made up of the Mirifle, Digil, and Rahanweyn the majority of which live in the Bay and Bakool between the Juba and

Shabelle rivers in southern Somalia. The Garre, Tunueg and Tunni are part of the Digil, and the Bagadi are considered as part of the Rahanweyn. Other minority groups include the Bantus (Jareer) in south central Somalia and the Bajunis, Barawanis, Benadit and Jaaji who live along the coast and are of Arab decent. The Sab (bondsmen of a pastoralist clan group) are usually discriminated by other nomadic Somalis, and consist of the Gabooye, Madhibaan, Muuse, Dharyo, Howlew, Hawraar, Yahhar, Galgalo, Boon and Habar Yaquup and Eyle. They are scattered in southern Somalia.[9] The Yibr who claim to be descendants to the biblical Hebrews live along the coast in Mogadishu in Basasso and Borama.

The Genesis of al Shabaab and its Operations

In 1991 anarchy ensued in Somalia after the expulsion of Said Barre. The Somali National movement (SNM) took control of the north, while the capital of Mogadishu and southern Somalia was under the control of the United Somalia Congress (USC).[10] On 26 January 1991 USC formed an interim government under Ali Mahdi Muhammed, which the SNM refused to recognize. In May 1991 SNM declared the northern Somali regions as independent, establishing the Republic of Somaliland. Subsequent fighting among rival faction leaders resulted in displacement, starvation and the deaths of thousands of Somalis, which led the United Nations to intervene. In August 1992, responding to the political chaos and humanitarian disaster, a UN relief effort called United Nations Operation in Somalia (UNOSOM I) was activated and dubbed "operation provide relief" that created an environment that enabled delivery of humanitarian assistance.

In December 1992 the United States joined the mission and it was named operation "restore hope". In March 1993, the UN changed the mission to UNOSOM II with more nations contributing forces and the US handing control over to the UN on 9th May 1993. On 3rd and 4th October 1993 the first battle for Mogadishu commonly referred to as "Blackhawk down" or the "Day of Rangers" by Somalis was fought in Mogadishu between forces of the United States, supported by UNOSOM II and Somali militia men loyal to the self proclaimed president to be Farah Aideed, who also had support from armed civilian fighters. The battle led to the deaths of eighteen American soldiers and over five hundred Somalis. The situation continued to deteriorate and in 1994 and 1995 the United States and the United Nation withdrew their forces from Somalia respectively.[11]

In June 1995 Aideed declared himself the president of Somalia but he was not recognized locally or internationally. On 1st August 1996 Aideed died of a heart attack due to an injury sustained on July 24th 1996 when he was attacked by Osman Ali and Ali Mahdi Mohammad, warlords who had been his allies. Ali Mahdi Muhammad was president under the United Somali Congress (USC) party from 29 Jan 1991 to 26 Jan 1997. After that Somalia remained without a president until a Transitional National Government (TNG) was formed on 27Aug 2000 to 14 October 2004 under Abdiqasim Salad Hassan. In October 2004, Abdullahi Yusuf Ahmed of the Somalia Salvation Democratic front (SSDF) took power when warlords had reached a power sharing agreement after having talks in Kenya. The agreement called for a 275 member parliament and Abdullahi Yusuf called for African peacekeepers to restore order within Somalia.[12]

5

In May 2006, fighting broke out in Mogadishu between the Transitional Federal Government (TFG) and the Islamic Courts Union (ICU), also known as the Union of Islamic Courts (UIC) or Supreme Islamic Courts Council (SICC) or Supreme Council of Islamic Courts. The ICU was formed in 2000 by former members of al Itihaad al Islamiya (AIAI) as the Union of Sharia Law Courts. These courts were created to administer justice in the districts where they had been established as a result of the absence of governance systems due to the prevailing chaos of the 1990s. Each court maintained a militia and eleven of these courts chose to pool their militia's resources in order to take control over Mogadishu.

The TFG sponsored warlords known as the Alliance for the Restoration of Peace and Counterterrorism (ARPCT) to oppose the courts. They engaged in fierce battles in June 2006 in which the ICU seized control of Mogadishu and much of southern Somalia.[13] By the end of 2006 the ICU had driven Yusuf's TFG to Baidoa. The situation then escalated and by early 2007 Ethiopian forces forced the UIC from Mogadishu.[14] Al Shabaab served as the military wing of the ICU and it began operating independently in early 2007. This group grew out of the Islamic Union (IU) or al Itihaad al Islamiya (AIAI) which sought to establish an Islamic state in the Horn of Africa. The presence of the Ethiopian military in Somalia rallied followers with the intention of fighting to rid Somalia of what it termed "foreign Invaders".

Earlier on in 7th December 2006 the United Nations Security Council adopted resolution 1725 that authorized the Intergovernmental Authority on Development (IGAD) to establish a protection and training mission in Somalia.[15] The resolution was implemented in January 2007 when the African Union Peace Security Council

6

authorized the deployment of the African Mission in Somalia (AMISOM) with the mandate to support transitional government structures, implementation of a national security plan, training of the Somali security forces, and assistance in creating a secure environment for the delivery of humanitarian aid.[16] The mission also supports the Transitional Federal Government's Forces against al Shabaab militants with a renewable six month mandate. In the months that followed the ICU was ejected from Mogadishu in early 2007. The ICU's moderate wing was led by Sheikh Sharif Sheikh Ahmed who embraced TFG and became TFG's president from 31 Jan 2009 to 20 August 2012 while affiliated with the alliance for the Re-Liberalization of Somali (ARS). He took over power from Adan Mohamad Nuur Madobe who was the interim president from 29 December 2008.

Al Shabaab Leadership

Al Shabaab's leadership is called the Shura Council.[17] The key members of this organization are Ahmed Abdi Godane (Mukhtar Abu Zubair) who is the leader (emir). He hails from Hargeisa in Somaliland and is of Isaaq clan. He studied in a madrassa in Pakistan and is a recluse and usually antagonistic. He believes in global jihad and draws his support from foreign fighters. Sheikh Mukhtar Robow (Abu Mansur) is the deputy leader and one of the original founders of al Shabaab and its former spokesman. He hails from Baidoa and is of Rahanweyn clan. He is a very influential figure who established the first militant training camp in 1996 in Huddur. He trained in Afghanistan with the Taliban and is committed to the implementation of his understanding of Sharia.

Ali Mohamed Rage (Ali Dhare) is the al Shabaab spokesman and hails from Hawiye clan in Banadir region. He is very vocal on issuing threats against neighboring countries. Hassan Dahir Aweys is a senior member and former leader of Hizbul Islam. He hails from Galgudud region and is a member of the Habar Gedir of Hawiye clan. He was the leader of the military wing of AIAI and co-founder of ARS with Sheikh Ahmed and supports the creation of a Sharia based state in Somalia. Faud Mohammud Qalaf (Shongole) is a senior member believed to be in charge of al Shabaab operations in Puntland. He hails from the Harti sub-clan of the Darood clan. He hates the media with a passion and refers to media organizations as agents of the infidel. Finally Ibrahim Hajji Jama Mead (Ibrahim al Afghani) is a senior leader and one of the founding members of Shabaab who hails from Somaliland's Habar Awal sub-clan of Isaaq clan. He has fought alongside al Qaeda in Kashmir and Afghanistan. He is an advocate of global jihad. This leadership profile is indicative of traits, qualities and experience of key al Shabaab leaders to demonstrate how they are able to influence its future operations and direction.

Al Shabaab Strategic Objectives

Al Shabaab's interests are a matter of speculation while the group's vision seems to be global jihad.[18] The strategic goal of the group remains to establish a Somali Islamic caliphate in the entire Horn of Africa, a nation-state for the "Quran".[19] Their intent is to win the support and galvanize the Somali people against the Americans, Ethiopians, Kenyans, Ugandans, AMISOM forces, and non-Muslims who are labeled as "crusaders". Some of al Shabaab's leadership, like Sheikh Mukhtar Robow, has shown interest in having the whole Somali nation under one flag. As a result, they want to gain political power by exploiting the current anarchy to control the whole of Somalia. Their long term dream is getting the northeastern province of Kenya and the Ogaden region of southeastern Ethiopia occupied by Ethiopian Somalis to realize their vision of Greater Somalia.

<u>Al Shabaab's Operational Concept</u>

Al Shabaab believes that only through the concept of Salafi-Jihadi ideology can they advance their agenda with propaganda that America is the cause of most of the tragedies that have befallen Muslims.[20] The merger with al Qaeda in early 2012 shows an increasingly global militant group which has earned international terror recognition with recruits from across the world from countries such as the Comoros, Kenya, Pakistan, Sudan, Sweden, Uganda, the US, the United Kingdom and Yemen among others. It is evident that its efforts are part of a global Jihadist struggle with the implication of global terror capability. Al Shabaab, just like other terrorist groups, has struck terror and caused anguish in the Horn of Africa region. Terrorist actions in Somalia, Kenya, Ethiopia and Uganda have led to the deaths of thousands of innocent civilians from these countries including AMISOM peace keepers based in Somalia.

This militia group was able to capture and control territory, sea ports and lines of communication like southern and central Somalia, the port city of Kisumayo, and Baidoa, which enabled it to have maneuver space to plan operations, mobilize and train recruits, and receive and generate resources to sustain their operations. Imposition of their strict version of Sharia Law in areas they have occupied and the formation of an administration to oversee the implementation of Sharia has been their mode of governance and allowed them to consolidate their grip on occupied communities. Administrative mechanisms include establishing district commissioners, heads of information, heads of security, heads of finance, and heads of preaching.

Al Shabaab has on occasion conducted selective attacks in the Kenya towns of Nairobi and Garissa, as well as conducted attacks in the Ugandan capital city of Kampala in July 2010. These actions were intended to show displeasure at regional countries involvement in Somalia by having deployed troops in Somalia whose objective would deny them freedom and space to train, plan and subsequently launch attacks for the purpose of furthering their strategic goals. Executions and flogging of law breakers publicly by al Shabaab is a tactic intended to cause fear to those opposed to their beliefs and a way of entrenching Sharia law, which is a decisive point along the line to their strategic goal of establishing a Somali Islamic caliphate. They have kidnapped government officers from the northeastern province of Kenya, Mule Yesse Edward, a local administrator and Fredrick Irungu, who works for the Ministry of Immigration, and they shot and killed David Tebbut and kidnapped his French wife Judith in the coastal tourist town of Lamu on 1October 2011. They have tried to use the hostages to demand the release of their captured militia and all Muslims held in Kenyan prisons, a demand that has not been honored since it's contrary to Kenya's position of non-negotiation with terrorist groups or organizations.[21]

The Strategic Situation of the Crises and Threat Posed To Kenya and the Region

Somalia is strategically located in the Horn of Africa with ties to other African countries, and close historical and religious links with both majority Islamic countries and Arab states. It's a member of both the UN and AU. Geographically it is predisposed to foreign Islamic jihadists and fighters from terror prone nations in the Middle East, especially Yemen and Afghanistan, by virtue of being a failed and predominantly Muslim state. The crisis in Somalia is of a strategic nature as it has gotten all the nations in the

Horn of Africa and the region involved fighting al Shabaab, participating in peacekeeping operations, or being accused of supporting al Shabaab. The situation has taken more than a decade and currently has affected and continues to affect millions of people within and outside of Somalia. The longevity of the conflict has had widespread implications for the region and Somali society. In spite of being a people with a common culture the Somalis remain divided.[22]

Serious crimes against humanity have been committed by this dangerous militia and violent clashes and confrontations continue to occur between them and AMISOM forces in what may turn into a complex insurgency if the gains by AMISOM forces are not maintained and supported. Women and children continue being the victims of the ongoing lawless situation through death, rape, and displacement. Journalists, aid workers, and hostages are often victims of al Shabaab's heinous acts of beheading.[23] Somalia has a new president and a young parliament as it emerges from a period of lawlessness. It still lacks democratic institutions and rule of law and has a volatile, uncertain, complex and ambiguous environment occasioned by al Shabaab that has led to kidnappings, the internal displacement of people, an outflow of refugees into neighboring countries, piracy in the Indian Ocean, hijacked ships and hostages still awaiting payment of ransom, poverty, unemployment, and unregulated trade and commerce. This enviroment has hindered the possibility of undertaking development projects and investment opportunities and increased the competition for meagre resources. Al Shabaab has extended its tentacles into the region to recruit and radicalize jobless youth to fill its rank and file and subsequently pursue its agenda.

The complex situation has threatened the relative peace and stability enjoyed in the region and the spillover effects including terror attacks and proliferation of small arms and light weapon to the region, present an intricate problem that is Somalia today, and if not addressed, poses a threat to Kenya and the entire Horn of Africa region.

Threat Posed To Kenya and the Region

Kenya and the Horn of Africa region at large still face a threat posed by al Shabaab as the militia outfit, though degraded by the KDF and AMISOM, still has the ways and means to pose a threat even though they were dislodged in September 2012 from their strongholds in southern Somalia including the Port of Kisumayo and Mogadishu respectively. In terms of financial resources, al Shabaab has lost import and export revenue due to the capture of the Port of Kisumayo by the KDF, which was their main source of income. Some Muslim nations working through proxy organizations that believe that they are obligated by Quranic orders to finance jihad are another source of financial support to al Shabaab.[24] The local religious leaders, mosques, and community networks also provide financial support for logistics and operations including provisions for sustenance.[25]

In manpower, it is estimated that between six thousand to seven thousand fighters make up al Shabaab[26] and it is estimated that between seven hundred and fifty to one thousand of them are foreign fighters.[27] These fighters are capable of using a wide range of weapon systems and equipment which includes assault rifles, hand grenades, explosives, machine guns, recoilless cannons, rocket propelled grenades (RPGs), anti-tanks rockets, and 60mm mortars. They use converted four wheel drive

Jeeps and Land cruisers mounted with anti-air craft machine guns known as technicals.[28]

The Threat Posed to Kenya

Kenya is a democratic nation that espouses rights and fundamental freedoms, such as the freedom of movement, association, expression, media, conscience, religion, belief, and opinion. It is a hub for international financial transactions and banking in the Horn of Africa and the region. It supports the neighboring countries in the delivery of humanitarian aid and relief assistance programs due to its infrastructure and serving as the headquarters for several International Non Governmental Organizations (INGOs), Non Governmental Organizations (NGOs), the United Nations Habitat and Regional Centre for the United Nations Higher Commission on Refugees, and the United Nations Environmental Program. The Mombasa seaport serves the neighboring land locked countries of Burundi, Ethiopia, Rwanda, South Sudan, and Uganda, including parts of the Democratic Republic of Congo. Kenya is also a world class tourist destination.

All these factors have opened up Kenya for foreign investment especially from the West. These qualities sometimes attract extremists who want to settle scores based on their own motive and agenda to move into the country and target Kenyan people and investments, both local and foreign. Any terrorist activities targeting Kenya constitute a threat to security and Kenya's national interest. These interests include the survival of Kenya as a free and independent nation with its fundamental values, way of life, prospering and intact institutions, as well as a healthy and growing free market economy that provides opportunities for individual prosperity and a resource base for other national endeavors. It also serves as a source for a stable and secure international and national environment, where political and economic freedom, human rights and democratic institutions flourish.[29] It's therefore imperative that threats to the Kenyan national interest from al Shabaab or any terrorist group shall be dealt with resolutely. This is one of the reasons that led to Kenyan troops pursuing al Shabaab insurgents into southern Somalia on 16 October 2011 in a joint operation with the transitional government forces.[30]

Al Shabaab has conducted terror attacks across the borders into Kenya, especially in Garissa and Eastleigh. There was a grenade attack on a church on 30 September 2012 that killed two children in Nairobi. On 18 November 2012 a bus bomb attack that killed six people in Eastleigh and a 1 July 2012 attack in Garissa at a church where seventeen people died. On 6th December 2012 another grenade attack killed three people and on 20 November 2012 three KDF soldiers were shot in Garissa. The targets of these terror attacks seem to be concentrated in Eastleigh, a Somali dominated town in Nairobi and Garissa, a Kenyan town at the center of the Kenya Somali community. Attacks on churches are an indication of intolerance to Christianity and a clear confirmation of of al Shabaab's pursuit of its strategic goal. Attacks in Eastleigh are to cause fear and despondency among Kenyan shoppers who go to shop in the busy and well stocked malls in this area of Nairobi. It is also a statement to Kenyan authorities that they are within reach of lucrative targets and that they are unable to protect their population. This is a clear challenge that presents the security organizations with an opportunity to reevaluate security strategy.

Small Arms, light weapons proliferation, and IEDs are a security dilemma posed by al Shabaab. Somalia has become the major source of most of the illegal arms in

14

Kenya, as they are smuggled cross the porous borders. The availability of these weapons lead to increasing insecurity, as well as increased incidents of cattle rustling and robbery with violence leading to the deaths of women and children, security agents and the raiders, injuries, loss of property and displacement of Kenyan citizens.[31] Currently there are over six hundred thousand illicit arms in circulation in the country, according to a survey conducted in Kenya on small arms by a Geneva based small arms survey group.[32] These weapons find their way into other countries, such as Uganda, Tanzania and the Democratic Republic of Congo leading to violent crimes in these countries too.

Another threat posed by al Shabaab is in the form of a weapon and method available to them and critical in terms of inflicting casualties, specifically the improvised explosive devices (IED). Al Shabaab will continue to use it against regional peacekeeping forces in Somalia and in attacks in countries that contribute troops to try and put pressure on these governments and public opinion to pull their forces out of Somalia. It is important for contributing countries to leverage and align efforts both within Somalia and in home countries by sharing information and intelligence.

The lack of institutions of governance in Somalia due to the menace of al Shabaab has created a breeding ground for pirates who frequently interfere with sea trade and commerce. This has led to increases in the cost of shipping due to increases in the cost of insurance and security escorts. As a result, the cost of imports went up, which affected the economies of Kenya and the region. This includes the global trade to and from Asia that uses these routes through the Indian Ocean. However, since AMISOM's capture and control of Kisumayo and Operation Atlanta conducted by the

European Union (EU) Naval Force to take disruptive action against pirate bases on shore, the rate of piracy has gone down in the Horn of Africa and off the Somali coast.[33]

During al Shabaab's control of south and central Somalia, contraband goods reportedly entered Kenya through the port city of Kisumayo via the border towns of Mandera, Liboi, and Hulugho before going to Garissa and then Eastleigh in Nairobi. An alternative route from Garissa would be via Modogashe, Garbatula, Isiolo or Meru then to Nairobi. The same routes are used for small arms and light weapons smuggling.[34] These are the preferred routes as some of the security agents in these areas are compromised and apathetic.

Kenya is currently hosting over four hundred and fifty thousand Somali refugees as a result of the insecure situation that al Shabaab has created in Somalia.[35] Their presence has brought about competition for resources with the local community, raised concerns about communicable diseases, environmental degradation due to firewood harvesting as the main source of energy, and competition for housing in urban areas. Refugee camps are a source of insecurity too, as they are havens for criminals who disguise themselves as refugees but once in the country, find their way out of the camps and move to the cities and towns where they engage in criminal and terrorist activities. The recent spate of grenade attacks in Nairobi was attributed to lack of proper registration and accountability of the recent influx of refugees. The result was xenophobic attacks on members of the Somali community after one of the attacks on a commuter bus.

Al Shabaab also poses a threat because they target refugee camps and mosques for recruitment of exploitable youth. Some radical Muslim clerics urge the youth to join. Eastleigh in Nairobi is one of the areas where agents recruit kids who end up going to join al Shabaab in Somalia to fight.[36] The main root causes for joining are unemployment, illiteracy, poverty, economic marginalization and ideology, strong brotherhood bonds, sense of belongings, reputation building, prospect of fame or glory, and social status benefits. Recruiters are able to entice their recruitment targets through the use of propaganda.[37] Some youth are made to believe that al Shabaab is fighting to maintain their values and way of life.[38] As a result these youth are radicalized and Islamized and become enemies of their own people by being sent back to attack targets at home. Several have been arrested from across all ethnic tribes and prosecuted.Money laundering using "hawala", an informal money transfer system, is the mode used by al Shabaab and Somalis to transact currency in Eastleigh and Nairobi. Within minutes of a transaction's completion, it finds its way to Somalia through the purchase of goods in Kenya and through the porous borders along the Kenya-Somalia border.[39] The government ends up losing tax revenue to this unorthodox monetary system of transfer that is not accountable in its dealings. The lack of transparency makes it impossible to develop a strategy for countering it, as transactions cannot be monitored or traced.

The kidnapping of two aid workers with Medicine San Frontiers in Sept 2011 from Dadaab refugee camp, the shooting and killing of the British tourist Tebbut, and the kidnapping of his French wife Judith in October 2011 from Lamu prompted the Kenyan authorities to react to these violations of its territorial integrity and pursue its national interests by sending troops across the border to secure and defend territorial integrity and deny al Shabaab freedom of movement and action. As a result of these types of

17

terrorist and criminal acts, the Kenyan tourism industry was negatively affected with a corresponding impact on Kenya's economy. This was too much to bear as tourism is Kenya's largest source of foreign revenue. It brings in approximately $500 million in annual earnings.[40] The impact of terrorism on tourism has a multiplier effect due to the loss of jobs, unemployment, and poverty.[41] This was infringing on Kenya's survival interests. It was for this reason that Kenya chose to act – in order to safe guard its interests at all cost.

Threat Posed to Uganda

Uganda was the first country to provide soldiers in 2007 by playing a vital role in propping up the transitional government. Support also came from the US and the international community through the African Union. As a result, Uganda is viewed as an enemy by al Shabaab. Since then, al Shabaab has targeted Uganda and on 11 July 2010 over seventy people were killed in two blasts in the Ugandan capital Kampala at a rugby club and at a restaurant as football fans watched the World Cup final.[42] The threat has also been extended in Somalia where Uganda has contributed the bulk of the force and has suffured the highest casualty numbers.[43]

Threat Posed to Ethiopia

Ethiopia's southeastern Ogaden region is inhabited by people of Somali origin, making them a lucrative target to be sought after by al Shabaab due to culture dynamics and in line with al Shabaab's goal of establishing a Somali Islamic caliphate. The Ogaden Somalis joining al Shabaab would pose a security threat to the Ethiopian government due to possibility of merging with the Ogaden National Liberation Front, a rebel group from the same region fighting the Ethiopian government through acts of

18

terror to form a separate state. In late December 2006 the TFG invited Ethiopia to help fight ICU from Mogadishu, a war that went on until Ethiopia withdrew in 2009. However, others viewed Ethiopia as invaders whose priorities was to maintain Eritrea's isolation in the region and then to ensure that armed groups opposing it internally do not find sanctuary in Somalia.[44] During the latest attempts to liberate Somalia from al Shabaab in 2011 to 2012, Ethiopian forces played a significant role fighting alongside pro TFG militias and managed to uproot al Shabaab fighters from the Baledweyne Hiran region in central Somalia.

Threat Posed to Eritrea

Eritrea is regarded as the country that has a soft spot towards al Shabaab in the Horn of Africa region. UNSCR 1907 adopted on December 23, 2009 imposed an arms embargo on Eritrea and travel bans on its leaders based on accusations that the Eritrean government of aiding al Shabaab in Somalia. Eritrea also reportedly refused to withdraw troops from its disputed border with Djibouti. Eritrea's involvement in the Somali conflict reduces its position in the region and isolates her. Supporting al Shabaab would be trying to crystallize its hostility with Ethiopia and Djibouti who both have played important roles in diminishing al Shabaab.

Threat Posed to Burundi and Djibouti

Both Burundi and Djibouti are troop contributing countries under AMISOM's mandate and as a result they are a target of al Shabaab. Burundi has four thousand five hundred troops and has had a significant number of casualties since deployment. Djibouti is yet to suffer causalities. Its people share the same culture, ethnicity, language, and a national border with the people of Somalia a likely indication of ethnic and religious dynamism at play. Currently it hosts Combined Joined Task Force Horn of Africa (CJTF HOA), an American counter terrorism force deployed to defeat transnational extremist groups in the region. Instability in Somalia could spill over into Djibouti disrupting peace and tranquility.

<u>Al Shabaab's Strengths and Weaknesses</u>

Al Shabaab's strengths lie in the ability to mobilize large numbers of fighters on short notice, recruit and employ foreign fighters based on the specialized skills and experience they bring to the organization, melt and blend into civilian populations, make and use improvised explosive devices (IEDs), use social media as the means of communication to propagate propaganda, disseminate information and recruit followers. Another source of al Shabaab's strengths is the ability to fundraise from Muslim charitable foundations, the Gulf States, and the Somali diaspora to finance and sustain its operations.[45]

These strengths must be targeted and through employing strategies that capture the across the spectrum of national elements of power: military, diplomatic, informational and economic. Al Shabaab's weakness is a lack of credibility and just cause as demonstrated through its conduct such as the unjustified terror activities, the whipping of women and public executions, forced marriages between Somali women and foreign fighters, and a lack of support from the people.[46] There is a need for AMISOM and its partners to exploit this weakness in order to win the war against the militia.

The Strategic Implications for Kenya and the Horn of Africa Region

The threat of terror attacks on Kenyan infrastructure would derail Kenya's security and have a major impact on Kenyan life in terms of trade, commerce, and development. This would likely lead to a loss of investors from the country and the subsequent negative impact on the overall regional investment opportunities, lack of job creation, poverty and unemployment. The Gulf of Aden and the Bab al Mandeb off the coast of Somalia are important strategic sea lines of commerce and communication as they are shipping routes that connect the Indian Ocean with the Mediterranean Sea through the Red Sea where over two thousand ships cross annually. Seven percent of world oil for consumption and thirty percent of European oil goes through these sea lines of commerce and communication. The threat of al Shabaab in HOA will impact commerce as the region will continue to be unstable, consequently becoming a breeding ground for pirates.

The interference of Somali pirates with these sea routes will affect global sea trade that flows through the Indian Ocean. This will lead to an increase in the cost of security escorts and the cost of insurance for the shipping industry. This in turn translates to a higher cost for imported products. It will also have a negative impact on the interests of the people in the region as they will be unable to realize and achieve their goals in such a hostile environment. Development in socio-economic sectors, infrastructure, electricity, water and sanitations, road construction, schools and hospitals will stagnate. Refugees will increase as people seek safer havens. An unstable Somalia would pull in both actors and spoilers within Somalia and from the region leading to a complex regional conflict that could destabilize the entire region and beyond.

The Kenyan Response

Kenya would like to promote democracy, security, peace and stability in the region as it is the regional hub of trade, commerce and information technology. Instability in the region would compromise the achievements across the entire socio-economic sector. That is why it supported TFG, has hosted refugees, and continues to play a part in providing peacekeeping forces. Kenya promotes opportunities and development for its people in order to create jobs to meet the youth bulge challenge, advance peace and security through agreements with its neighbors by encouraging bilateral and multilateral military exercises. It also promotes economic growth through regional economic partnership and establishing trading blocks in order to pull up weaker economies and ensure fair trading practices amongst member states to create opportunities for its people and eradicate poverty.

Kenya has also passed anti-terrorism legislation known as the counter-terrorism financing bill, which will regulate financial transactions and stop money laundering. It will also make it an offence for any individual or organization to open, operate, finance, recruit or assist any person or organization engaged in terrorist activities. The law will also ensure effective prosecution of terrorists and their agents. Kenya also has an established counter terrorism centre where it trains its personnel from all security agencies in order to competently address the emerging terror threats and trends.

The Kenya Defense Forces have been on the fore front in fighting al Shabaab and effectively dislodging them from their strongholds in southern Somalia as part of the Global War on Terror. The Kenyan Navy has been actively involved in counter piracy operations in the nation's economic exclusion zone and beyond to ensure freedom of navigation and denial of access to the pirates.

In addressing the refugee challenges the Ministry of Immigration is working in liaison with UNHCR as part of the interagency cooperation and coordination to ensure the observation of international conventions in regard to refugees without compromising security. The government through banks and financial institutions is offering the women and youth interest free funds for loans in order to undertake income generating projects as a way of promoting small scale enterprises and poverty eradication. The Kenyan leadership is adhering to good governance and accountability to ensure security forces are well trained and properly resourced to be able to effectively deal with emerging security challenges. They are also involved with capacity building to tackle the ever changing security threats by embracing new technologies, including those intended to deter cyber crime. Kenyan leadership has also embarked on an interagency counter terrorism program, as well as information sharing in order to identify and effectively target terrorists; especially terrorist group leadership. Finally, Kenya is also encouraging military leaders to discuss issues and conduct joint counter terrorism exercises and training with allies and partners like exercise Natural Fire with US AFRICOM and other East African nations as a way of sharing knowledge, building trust, and shaping the region.

Conclusion: the Regional Challenges of Somalia and the Way Ahead

As the regional partners through AMISOM confront the threats that al Shabaab poses and turn them into challenges and those challenges into opportunities, the main challenges that the region faces will remain within and related to Somalia. While al

23

Shabaab has lost ground and must be eliminated in order to stabilize Somalia. One of the first things that must be addressed is the lack of trust among some of the regional states; especially those perceived to have been supporting al Shabaab like Eritrea and many of the Arab Gulf states. The challenge of manpower and logistics must also be addressed. It will be necessary for regional actors to be able to adequately resource their endeavors to stabilize all of Somalia. It is not enough just to secure towns. In order to be successful in dealing with the threats that originate from within Somalia it is necessary to engage and pacify the entire country to prevent al Shabaab from establishing bases in remote areas and using them to plan and launch attacks. It is also important to get accurate and timely information on the enemy to enable effective responses. Finally the Regional armies' divergent interests must be mitigated in order to not negatively affect the coalition's cohesion and the ability to conduct operations.

As a military specialist, it is important to develop and employ instruments of national power in a synchronized and integrated way in a joint, intergovernmental, interagency, and multinational manner by balancing ways and means to achieve a stable Somalia as the key to achieving security and establishing enduring peace, stability, and prosperity in the region. I recommend that diplomatically, the United Nations, AU, and the international community should call upon all regional countries who are stake holders, including the Arab Gulf states, to support the newly elected Somali government. It is necessary for the international community and the regional actors should open diplomatic missions in Mogadishu. Information sharing should also be encouraged among the regional partners and the coalition forces participating in PSO. Communication efforts and messaging should be established and conducted through use of print and electronic media. The effort of winning hearts and minds should be undertaken and media broadcasts should be leveraged to win the support of the Somali citizenry. Regional and Somali national governments should continue to counter al Shabaab's propaganda. There should be increased and better coordinated information sharing and coordination of intelligence among the coalition forces in support of regional counter terrorism efforts.

Militarily, I recommend that the UN and the US continue the logistical support to and resourcing of AMISOM Forces. The UN should take over the mission from the AU Forces in order to broaden it and give it a true international legitimacy. This will increase the opportunities to build capacity for the development of effective security institutions and the establishment of the rule of law. AMISOM Forces should embark on training and building capacity for SNG forces in order to start conducting effective security duties based on a time line. The armed Somali groups should be encouraged to demobilize, disarm, and reintegrate themselves into Somali society by offering skills training, as well as using monetary incentives as a non-lethal approach. US Africa Command should encourage military to military dialogue and partnership in training and partner capacity building. The regional militaries need to develop and establish a robust, but well trained and equipped small team units that are mission oriented with special operations capability to counter the emerging threats.

Economically, the regional and international development institutions - the Department For International Development, the European Union, the Inter-Governmental Authority on Development, the International Monetary Fund, the NGO Community, the UN including the United Nations Development Program, the US Agency for International Development, and the World Bank should support the new SNG with financial support to enable the running of the government departments and programs and ensure proper monetary discipline. The regional nations should admit Somalia into the regional economic and trading blocks to encourage regional trade and provide a market for its products to enable its economy to pick up.

The current efforts to mitigate the threats originating from within Somalia include the current peace support operations being conducted by AMISOM that are mandated by UN Security Council resolution (UNSCR) 1725 of 6 December 2006. In December 2009 the UN voted for an embargo on Eritrea for training and arming al Shabaab and in Jan 2012 passed UNSCR 2036 to mandate AMISOM to take all necessary measures to reduce the threat posed by Al Shabaab. Other efforts are the election of Speaker of Parliament Mohammed Osman Tawaari, and President Hassan Sheikh Mohamud on 16 Sep 2012 and the European Union (EU) Naval efforts to patrol Somali waters to counter piracy and allow for the free flow of commerce and trade, as well as to further clear the sea lanes of communications and guarantee safe passage of ships and goods.

It will also be necessary to train troops before deployment and educate law enforcement in order to broaden the understanding of how to prevent, detect, protect and respond to improvised explosive devices (IEDs) and vehicle borne improvised explosive devices (VBIEDs). By securing borders and training border patrol personnel in more effective security measures and the screening of refugees it will be possible to separate out the criminal element from the legitimate refugees before they can be registered and find their way into Kenya through the refugee camps. It is also necessary to increase job opportunities for Somali youth, which will reduce their exploitability by al

26

Shabaab. The current achievements by the international community and AMISOM forces are commendable; however they are not an end by themselves. The threat from al Shabaab is likely to remain moderate in the region despite the gains achieved. However, it should lessen as democratic institutions and the rule of law begin to take shape in Somalia and as challenges affecting the larger part of the region's population and communities are attended to. These gains can be achieved through governmental, bilateral, and multilateral approaches that are inclusive of regional governments, the international community, nongovernmental organizations, and the private sector in order to realize opportunities presented for Kenya and regional partners and build a secure and prosperous region.

Endnotes

[1] Stephanie Hanson, "Al Shabaab," August 10, 2011. http:www.cfr.org/Somalia/al-Shabaab/p18650 (accessed December30, 2012).

[2] Central Intelligence Agency World Fact Book, "Africa Somalia," November 2012, http://www.ciaguo/library/publications/the world Fact book / gors/so.html, (accessed December 30, 2012).

[3] Ken Menkhans, Governance without Government in Somalia. International security, volume 31, no 3 (winter 2006/07), 74.

[4] Ministry of Planning and Statistics, "Puntland Facts and Figures" 2003 1st Edition, 9.

[5] Macmillan World Atlas.

[6] Central Intelligence Agency Fact Book, https://www.cia.gov/library/publications/the-world-factbook/geos/so.html (accessed Mar 6, 2013).

[7] Ibid.

[8] Joakim Gundel, Clans in Somalia, Report on a lecture COI workshop Vienna, May 15, 2009 (revised edition) December 2009, 7-12.

[9] Ibid., 12-15.

[10] Global security .org, "Somalia Civil War", www.globalsecurity.org/military/world/war/somalia.htm (accessed December 27,2012).

[11] Ibid.

[12] Ibid., 1.

[13] Ibid., 2.

[14] David Shinn, "Al Shabaab Foreign Threat to Somalia", *Foreign Policy Research Institute*, Spring 2011, 206.

[15] United Nations, "Security Council Approves African Protection Training Somalia", Dec 2006 www.un.org/News/Press/docs/2006/sc8887.doc.htm (accessed December 27,2012).

[16] United Nations Security Council Resolution 1772, S-RES-1772 (2007), 3.

[17] Nathaniel Horadam, "Al Shabaab leadership profiles", Critical Threats, August 3, 2012. www.criticalthreats.org/somalia/al-shabaab-leadership, (accessed Jan 5, 2013).

[18] Ken Menkhans, "Conflict Analysis Somalia", October 2012, 26.

[19] Shabaab Al-Mujahedeen Movement Declaration, "A New Praise Worthy Terrorism Campaign In Response To The Tyrant America" April 5, 2008.

[20] Ibid., 2.

[21] Somali Al Shabaab Rebels Threaten to Kill Kenyan Hostages. *A Reuters report*, www.nbcnews.com/id/50566711/ns/world_news-europe (accessed Mar 8, 2013).

[22] Nuruddin Farah,Roland Marchai,Asha Hagi, "Somalia ,A Nation Without A State", *The Nordic African Institute* Oct-Nov 2007.

[23] Al Shabaab Valentines Day Beheading of Mansuur Mohammed, www.bestgore.com/beheading/al-shabab-valentines-day-beheading (accessed. Mar 8, 2013).

[24] Michael Taamby, "Recruitment of Islamic Terrorist in Europe, Trends and Perspective" A report by Danish Ministry of Justice Jan14, 2005.

[25] Ibid.

[26] Ibid.

[27] Catherine Herridge, "Ranks of Somali Terror Group Swelling with Foreign Fighters". Nov 17,2011 http://www.foxnews.com/world /2011/11/17/ranks-somali-terror-group-swelling-with-foreign-fighters-including-americans/, (accessed Jan 1, 2012).

[28] Harmony Database, Counter Terrorism Centre. West Point. http://www.ctc.edu./harmony/harmony_docs.asp.

[29] The Republic of Kenya, the Constitution of Kenya, May 6,2010 chap. 2, 15-31.

[30] Somali Islamist Threaten Kenya, *The guardian,* October 17, 2011, http://www.guardian.co.uk/world/2011/oct/17/somali-islamists-threaten-kenya-attack. (accessed Mar 8, 2013)/

[31] Manasseh Wepundi, Ryana Murray, Eliud Thiga,and Anna Alvaazz del Frate, "Availability of Small Arms and Perceptions of Security in Kenya, an Assessment", *Special Report* ,June 2012, 54-55.

[32] Elizabeth Were, "Kenya 600,000 illicit Arms circulating within Kenya", http;//www.thestar.co.ke/news/article-14412/600,000-illicit-arms-circulating-withinkenya-reveals.(accessed December 29,2012).

[33] Operation Atlanta Somalia, May 15,2012, http://maritimesecurity.asia/free-2/operation-atalanta-somalia/eu-naval-force-delivers-blow-against-somali-pirates-on-shoreline-2/, (accessed 8 mar 2013).

[34] International crisis group, "Somalian Islamist", *Africa Report Number 100,* December 12 2005.

[35] 2012 UNHCR, Country Operations Profile-Kenya, www.**unhcr**.org/pages/49e483a16.html, (accessed Feb 20,2013).

[36] How Kenya's Little Mogadishu Became Hub for Somali militants, *The Christian monitor* http;//www/csmonitor.com/world/Africa/2009/0826/p06s02-woaf.html/, (accessed Feb 20,2013).

[37] Combating Terrorism Center at West Point. *CTC sentinel*, August 2012 volume 5, issue 7, 18-19.

[38] Ibid., 19.

[39] Ibid.

[40] Stafan Lovgren, "Terrorism Taking Toll on Kenya's Tourism Industry", *National Geographic News,* June 17, 2003.

[41] Ibid.

[42] BBC News. "Somali link in as 74 world cup fans die in Uganda blast", 12 July 2010, http://www.bbc.co.uk/news/10593771, (accessed Feb 20,2013).

[43] Uganda Peace Keeping Troops Dead in Somalia, http://www.timeslive.co.za/africa/2012/10/31/2700-ugandans-troops-dead-in-somalia-official,(accessed (Mar 5, 2013).

[44] Nuruddin Farah, Roland Marchai, Asha Hagi, "Somalia A Nation without a State", *The Nordic African Institute,* Oct-Nov 2007.

[45] Abu Mansoor Al –Amriki, "The beloved mujahidin in particular and the Muslim in general", January 08, 2008.

46 David Shinn, "Al Shabaab Foreign Threat to Somalia" Spring 2011, 209-214.

www.ingramcontent.com/pod-product-compliance
Lightning Source LLC
Chambersburg PA
CBHW080749290526
45790CB00008B/3389